JON FEENSTRA

TTL 6

WW2 VEHICLES

THROUGH THE LENS

PeKo Publishing Kft.

8360 Keszthely, Bessenyei György utca 37., Hungary

Email: info@pekobooks.com

www.pekobooks.com

Author: Jon Feenstra

ISBN: 978-615-6602-50-3

ACKNOWLEDGEMENTS

Finishing a book such as this always provides me with a great sense of accomplishment, and I appreciate Peter Kocsis continuing to allow me to do it for Peko. I enjoy trying to put the pieces together interpreting previously seen photographs in a new way or seeing new photos that add a new piece of the puzzle to the vast subject such as this. Thanks to a few long-time friends like Tom Cockle and Ron Volstad that are always there to provide an opinion on my interpretations of various things, and the encouragement and support from family - my fiancée Sandy, brother Greg and parents John and Helen, and my beautiful children Jessica and Ian.

CONTENTS

1. TYP 82 KFZ.1 „KÜBELWAGEN"

Like the American Jeep, the German Volkswagen Typ 82 Kfz.1 "Kübelwagen" (Kraftfahrzeug 1 / Motor Vehicle 1 "Bucket Car") was one of the most ubiquitous soft-skin vehicles throughout the war, produced from August 1940 until the plant was overrun by the British in April 1945. This long period means there were numerous detail differences throughout production. This Afrika Korps vehicle was produced between late 1940 and late 1941, with short rear mudguards, direction indicators on the windshield side, horn mounted in front of the driver's door, long door beads and early door handles, no hole for the jack below the doors, and the shovel mount on the driver's side (but missing the actual shovel here). To help distribute ground pressure and thus increase traction in soft ground Kronprinzenrad 200-12 wheels are mounted with Ballonsandreifen (balloon sand tires), the front one missing its hubcap. The plastic and fabric side windows are installed to presumably keep the dust down. On the fender is a regimental command pennant in what appears to be the black-white-black colors of an infantry unit.

This captured Kübelwagen is being used as an airfield runabout somewhere in Tunisia in 1943. The white star on blue background with yellow outline matches the marking on the C-47 Dakota behind it exactly. This vehicle has the same production features as the previous photo, including large diameter headlights that were used until late 1943. Unusually, the horn has been turned sideways. Jerrycan racks are mounted on both front and rear mudguards and once again the shovel is missing above the front mudguard. Clearly visible here is the external lead for the windshield wipers, a feature that was not changed until early 1944.

Unlike the previous two photographs, this Kübelwagen is equipped with the standard wheels and tires. It is an early 1942 production model with lengthened rear mudguards but still lacking the hole below the doors for the insertable "Wagenheber" (car jack), instead being equipped with a scissors-type jack. It also has the early spare tire mount with stiffening beads extending almost to the edge of the body panel. The spare wheel has the bar and padlock for securing against theft. In order to mount the jerrycans, the crew has relocated the horn beside the spare tire and the shovel to the rear panel, the handle of which is blocking the rear door. Notice the fabric blackout covers on the large headlights. On the front mudguard is the white helmet insignia, outlined in black, for Infanterie-Division (mot.) "Grossdeutschland", along with an unusual early style tactical symbol for what appears to be the headquarters of an artillery battery. On the door is the black loading label with "Kfz. 1" clearly visible at the top.

The Archive of Modern Conflict

Visible below the doors of this Kübelwagen is the round opening for the insertable car jack and the spare tire mount is the late version with shortened stiffening beads. Given that "WH-1429420" is painted in RAL 7021 Dunkelgrau and, despite the lack of markings, has been attributed to schwere Panzerabteilung 503, this vehicle was produced in late 1942 or very early in 1943. The horn is now mounted in front of the left side headlight and the later style of direction indicators can also be seen mounted on a tubular frame, further indications of this production period. On the edge of the mudguards are the tire pressure ratings "1.6 atu" in white, but Kübelwagens were seen with values ranging from 0.8 to 1.8 atu, with 1.4 seeming to be the most common.

The Archive of Modern Conflict

This Kübelwagen was also produced in late 1942 or very early in 1943, given that it still has the early, large diameter headlights and direction indicators, but lacks the front bumper rod that was installed between the front tow hooks in February/March 1943. It appears to be painted in the late Tropen colors of RAL 8020 Gelbbraun and RAL 7027 Graugrün although it could also have been re-painted RAL 7028 Dunkelgelb over the factory-applied RAL 7021 Dunkelgrau. Notice that the two front wheels have military pattern tires, whereas the spare is a civilian pattern with less aggressive tread. Behind the Kübelwagen is an Opel Blitz Allrad-Typ 3.6-6700A all-wheel drive truck, already displaying some of the production simplifications like elimination of the Opel Blitz logo on the front grille and deletion of the driver's spotlight.

This is another late 1942 production vehicle, still with the early spare tire mount with long stiffening beads but with a hole for the insertable jack. The hole was placed at the center of gravity such that the entire side of the Kübelwagen could be lifted. Once again, different tires are being used with the front two and spare having one style of military tread pattern, whereas the rear one has another. It is most likely painted in RAL 8020 Gelbbraun given that it is pictured in Tunisia, obviously captured by Americans if the graffiti is any indication! Presumably, "S-1" stands for the Personnel Section of a HQ unit. The "3" would seem to be a German marking, quite unusual given that the 3 was masked off and then a white patch haphazardly applied. Notice the grab handle and padlock securing the rear door, very rare features only seen on a select few Kübelwagens.

Given that the rims were different sizes, it is highly unusual to see a Kübelwagen equipped with both standard and balloon tires as seen here. Fitting balloon tires required an adjustment to the front axle as well, so this could explain the use of standard tires at the front. The spare tire mount also required an extension to secure a balloon tire to it. This vehicle has all the features of a very early 1943 production vehicle, with late spare tire mount but no front bumper rod and still finished in a very dusty RAL 7021 Dunkelgrau. Late style direction indicators and early large headlights are visible as well. It is equipped with an antenna mount, but this is not a purpose built Kfz.2 Funkwagen (radio car), of which a very small number were produced.

Very early in the 1943 production, starting at body number 15,371, a 20mm (3/4") diameter front bumper rod was added, bolted between the front tow hooks. This was fitted until body number 29,001 produced in late 1943 or early 1944, at which time it was discontinued. This corresponds to Wehrmacht registration numbers between approximately 1 430 000 and 1 635 000, so this Kübelwagen with license number "WH-1484282" falls within that series and the bumper is visible here although it blends in very well. It still mounts the large diameter headlights though, so was probably built in February or March 1943 given its RAL 7028 Dunkelgelb finish. Once again, we see two different tires patterns, civilian style on the right front and left rear, and military style for the left front and spare. After three different styles of horn, the final standard issue item was made by Hella with its typical "3-prong" face. Notice the "80 km" stencilled in black above a very worn load label on the driver's door, presumably indicating the maximum speed of 80 km/hr.

Despite its light weight of only 725 kg (1600 lbs.), a Kübelwagen could still get hopelessly stuck as these soldiers have discovered. Along with the front bumper rod seen in the previous photo, a rear bumper assembly was also added at body number 15,371, so this is a late 1942 or very early 1943 production vehicle as no bumper is present. It was also factory finished in RAL 7021 Dunkelgrau given the inside of the engine compartment and rear passenger door. Mounted on the engine compartment door are a tire pump and engine starting crank and the end of the insertable jack is just visible to the lower left of the 25.5hp engine. On the other side of the engine is the standard issue sheet metal toolbox stored on edge with some of its paint worn off.

After all else failed, they have now found some different "motive" power to give their Kübelwagen a pull. It appears to have been repainted in RAL 7028 Dunkelgelb with a camouflage of RAL 6003 Olivgrün and the mudguard edges are painted white for nighttime visibility. Another identifier of pre-1944 vehicles is the sheet metal license plate, which was eliminated late in 1943 with the registration number simply painted directly on the engine compartment door. With the engine cover closed we can now see that this vehicle with registration number "SS 212 905" carries the "sun wheel" marking in black for SS-Division "Wiking". Like all three branches of the Wehrmacht – Heer (army), Luftwaffe (air force) and Kriegsmarine (navy) – the Waffen-SS used the Kübelwagen extensively on all fronts.

Péter Kocsis

This Kübelwagen seen in Ostrowiec, Poland during 1944 has two features that suggest it was one of the final vehicles built with the front and rear bumpers at the end of 1943 or beginning of 1944. The front bumper is visible, but the rear license plate and blackout taillight cannot be seen which suggests that the sheet metal plate was deleted and the light relocated onto the engine compartment door, these changes occurring in this timeframe as well. The small diameter headlights are mounted with their visible electrical lead coming out of the back, whereas the windshield wiper external lead has been eliminated, both features introduced in late 1943 production. It appears to be painted in three-color camouflage of RAL 7028 Dunkelgelb, RAL 6003 Olivgrün and RAL 8017 Rotbraun. There is a small illegible white tactical symbol on the mudguard.

Sitting in front of "Wehrmacht Kino I" (Wehrmacht Cinema I) in 1944, this Kübelwagen finished in solid RAL 7028 Dunkelgelb displays all the features of a typical late 1943/early 1944 production vehicle, including front and rear bumpers (only the upturned exhaust pipe is visible here that was modified as such to accommodate the rear bumper), shovel still mounted, late style headlights, no direction indicators and lack of the external windshield wiper lead. "WH-1571 201" has the unit symbol for Werfer Regiment 82, a black S on a white shield outlined in black, on the front mudguard and a black load label on the driver's door, although the label has been uniquely applied by putting a break in it for the door bead, rather than painting over it as was typically done.

The Archive of Modern Conflict

Pictured undergoing maintenance at the unit workshop, this is the same vehicle seen in the previous photograph, now with its side windows fitted. The Sd.Kfz.2 Kettenkraftrad on the right, which appears to still be painted RAL 7021 Dunkelgrau, has the Werfer Regiment 82 emblem on its fender. Just visible on the rear of the Kübelwagen is the bracket for the bumper. Also visible below the rear edge of the roof tarpaulin is the sheet metal cover over the ventilation grille, which was introduced to help keep dust from building up behind the grille and causing the air-cooled engine to fail. This cover was not part of any production batch and could be retrofitted to any Kübelwagen, although it became standard later in the war. Notice above the soldier that the windshield has now suffered a rock, bullet or shrapnel strike and is cracked.

Amazingly, this is the same Kübelwagen seen in the previous two photographs, as evidenced by the license plate number, uniquely painted load label, and crack in the windshield. Camouflage has now been added with RAL 6003 Olivgrün and in the process the unit emblem has been painted over on the left mudguard. However, on the right mudguard is a black tactical symbol for a towed Nebelwerfer battery, confirming its attachment to Werfer Regiment 82. Notice that the nearest tire has now been replaced with one with a different tread pattern and the shovel has been removed or lost. Even in 1944, the Wehrmacht still needed horsepower, as evidenced by the supply column of wagons moving in the background.

A final picture of the same Kübelwagen, the camouflage over the load label matching the previous photograph as does the driver and soldier sitting on the windshield edge, who are the previous passenger and driver respectively. It is interesting to see the roof tarpaulin also camouflaged with RAL 6003 Olivgrün, which was unusual, as are the wheel rims. This photo finally provides a view of the rear bumper, as well as the final style of rear body features, the blackout taillight mounted on the engine compartment cover and the deleted sheet metal license plate. Notice the Gefreiter chevron on the sleeve of the soldier to the right, roughly equivalent to a British lance corporal.

This Luftwaffe Kübelwagen with license number "WL-528 097" has an unusual mix of features. It lacks the external windshield wiper lead and although the rod itself is missing, the front tow hooks appear to have the hole in them for the bumper attachment bolts. However, it also has the larger, early headlights and the roof tarpaulin is of the earlier type with only two support struts instead of three. Production most likely occurred in early-to-mid 1943. Behind the Kübelwagen is a 1938/39 Ford V8 3-ton truck manufactured in the USA, so most likely captured during the invasion of France and the low countries. To the right is an Italian Lancia 3Ro with license number "WH-1659708", many of which were absorbed into the Wehrmacht after Italy's capitulation. The photo was presumably taken in Italy in late 1943 or 1944.

These three American soldiers appear to be enjoying their captured Kübelwagen, finished in three-color camouflage with some interesting markings on the door, a white "12" above a Roman numeral "II". Given how freshly applied they look compared to the illegible unit symbol on the left mudguard, these could have been applied by the captors. Although much is missing from this vehicle, there are enough features to indicate an early 1944 production. The small hole for the electrical lead is behind the headlight mount indicating it was equipped with the later, smaller diameter headlights, and the clamp for the shovel is just visible, which wasn't eliminated from production until late 1944. It also has the late windshield clips which eliminated the cone-shaped rubber stop. The bumper rod is much smaller in diameter then was normally fitted, so it could be a field addition. The windshield also has only one wiper motor present, and although there was some late war vehicles produced with only one wiper, this one simply appears to be missing as the electrical lead is still visible.

This abandoned Waffen-SS Kübelwagen is being inspected by Americans during the Ardennes offensive in late 1944. The license plate "SS-156196" is quite interesting since it appears to have been painted over another one and then the two middle digits corrected. The lack of front bumper and late headlights indicate it was probably produced in the second half of 1944. Notice the holes for the missing windshield wipers and that it once again mounts different tires. Of particular interest is the driver's side tire, which is the wider tire (with associated rim) typically seen on the Typ 166 Schwimmwagen, the Kübelwagen's amphibious stablemate.

Three Kübelwagens, the nearest one with its roof up, sit amongst a vast array of German vehicles in a salvage yard, including a Kettenkrad, Sd.Kfz.11 halftrack, Sd.Kfz.251 Ausf.D halftrack, Sd.Kfz.261 kleiner Panzerfunkwagen (small armored radio car) and Steyr 1500A. The Kübelwagen in the middle lacks the shovel mount, an austerity measure introduced in late 1944. There also appears to be no indication that it ever had windshield wipers installed, or at least the motors themselves. Both vehicles have their stowage box covers open behind the rear seat and clearly visible is the crossbar behind the front seats that had clips for four rifles. The middle Kübelwagen is missing its fuel tank cap. The information contained in the black load label is, from top to bottom: "Kfz. 1", "Leergewicht 0.76 t" (Empty Weight in tonnes), "Nutzlast 0.45 t" (Payload in tonnes) and "Ve. Kl. II" (Vehicle Klasse II / Load Class II).

National Archives

As noted by the sign on the stair handrail, this Kübelwagen is being used by the 282nd Engineer Combat Battalion, attached to the XII US Army Corps and only arriving in France in December 1944, so this photo was taken some time in the spring of 1945. This is a very late production vehicle, lacking the shovel mount and only equipped with a single windshield wiper for the driver. It is also missing the interior crossbar, but this may have simply been removed. It is finished in overall RAL 7028 Dunkelgelb, with no markings visible, although someone has stuck a German mine marker flag, yellow with a black skull and crossbones, in the face of the horn. Behind the Kübelwagen is a Jeep complete with bumper mounted wire cutter and to the right is a Mercedes 170V saloon car.

Péter Kocsis

When the Pz.Kpfw.VI Ausf.H1 (subsequently named Tiger Ausf.E and then Tiger I) was introduced in the fall of 1942, the Panzerwaffe's combat potential increased exponentially given the Tiger's potent 8.8 cm Kw.K.36 (L/56) gun and near impenetrable armor. The vehicle shown here was produced in January 1943, still equipped with the K.F.F.2 twin driver's periscopes as per the holes above the view port but it has the triangular reinforcement plate at the front of the track guard and the over-sized Gepäckkasten (baggage bin) on the rear of the turret. Tiger "2" is one of nine issued to 13.Kompanie, Panzer-Regiment "Grossdeutschland" in February 1943 and these Tigers were delivered in the second Tropen scheme of RAL 8020 Braun with a disruptive pattern of RAL 7027 Grau, or possibly the first Tropen scheme. At some point in April 1943, the company changed its turret marking system to single and double digits as seen here, in white outline only. The turret Nebelwurfgerät (smoke candle dischargers) have been removed from their bracket, a common feature of GD's Tigers, as were the unditching logs carried on the side during Operation Zitadelle. Notice the gouge from a hit on the mantlet.

Péter Kocsis

These two Tigers are from 4.Kompanie, SS-Panzer-Regiment 3 (SS-Panzer-Grenadier-Division "Totenkopf"), seen on 21 February 1943 in a village along the Karlovka-Krasnograd road during the advance to re-take Kharkov. Both were built in January 1943 and were part of the nine Tigers received by the unit in the same month. Like GD's vehicles, they were also delivered in one of the Tropen schemes but repainted in a solid coat of whitewash with solid black turret numbers and a Balkenkreuz in black with a white outline. To the right is most likely "413", with the distinctive shape of the 3, and to the left is possibly "411", its stablemate in the 1.Zug (platoon), which also has the name "Fridel" on the forward turret side. Despite being virtually brand new and not yet having been in combat, both vehicles already have bent and battered track guards and 411 is missing two outer road wheels on the first and fifth torsion arms.

This Tiger I was built in late April/early May 1943 as it has the spare tracks mounted on the turret sides but still has the original drum cupola. It was one of seven vehicles delivered to 1.Kompanie/schwere. Panzer-Abteilung 502 in early June, seen here undergoing maintenance in their Tosno workshop area near Leningrad. While this company remained on the Russian front through the first half of 1943 attached to Armeeoberkommando 18 (A.O.K.18), the other two companies were rebuilding in France before re-uniting in early July. During this period 1.Kp. used a two-digit numbering system, "34" in solid white designating the 4th vehicle in the 3rd platoon (zug), before reverting to the standard 3-digit system when s.Pz.Abt.502 was whole again. This Tiger would have been delivered painted in solid RAL 7028 Dunkelgelb, to which the crew has added a disruptive pattern of RAL 6003 Olivgrün and RAL 8017 Rotbraun. Notice the S-Minenwerfer (S-Mine dischargers) on the front and rear corners, and the engine deck with open hatch lying to the rear of the tank. To the right is an Sd.Kfz.9/1 "Famo" with 6-ton Bilstein crane still finished in RAL 7021 Dunkelgrau and in the background is one of the rare early 15-ton Fries Strabokran, both of which were assigned to the Panzer Werkstattkompanie (maintenance company) of the unit.

“02” is another tank from 1.Kp./s.Pz.Abt.502, in this case the second Tiger in the Stabskompanie (headquarters company) assigned to the company executive officer/assistant commander. “01” was the commander’s tank. Like the previously seen "34", this vehicle has the spare track holders on the turret and thus is another late April/early May 1943 build and was also delivered in early June. All the Tigers in 1.Kp. had their Feifel air filters and track guards removed, the latter obviously done before the camouflage was applied if these two pictures are any indication. The crew has also removed the two headlights and ball mounted MG 34, no doubt stored inside the tank. Other visible production changes implemented in early 1943 included the deletion of the holes above the driver’s vision port for the K.F.F.2 twin periscope and the front face of the drive sprocket hub being machined flat.

This photo provides a good view of the Fiefel air filters mounted on the rear, in this case the later version with a simplified upper chamber design introduced in March 1943. The Tiger was produced in May 1943 since it lacks the rear frames that were welded to the hull for mounting the rear mudflaps, but still has the original turret with drum cupola and Nebelwurfgerät. This appears to be another Tiger from Panzer-Regiment "Grossdeutschland", which typically removed the smoke dischargers from their turret bracket, and the Balkenkreuz placement is consistent with GD. There is also a tactical number on the forward turret side that seems to be "01" in solid black, with the 1 having a long tail, also indicative of this regiment. It could possibly be "S01" or "A01" from the battalion staff or 9.Kompanie. It is finished in solid RAL 7028 Dunkelgelb and the picture was probably taken in late July or August 1943. Notice the flexible hose for refueling wrapped around the turret Gepäckkasten and the standard tube mounted on the upper hull side for a spare antenna rod.

Despite being stripped for parts, enough is still visible to indicate that this is a Tiger I probably built in December 1942. While the track guards are missing, the mounting blocks are all still present and clearly show the early style that had a bend in the middle to follow the profile of the hull, which transitioned to the later, straight style sometime later in December. The front hull extensions are also present to better accommodate the tow shackles, which has been documented as occurring at or about Fahrgestellenummer (Fgst Nr.), or chassis number, 250055 also built sometime in December. The Tiger is from 2.Kp./s.Pz.Abt.503, although the solid white turret number "211" appears to have a slightly different shape to the "2" that was a trademark of 2.Kompanie. A faded and worn Balkenkreuz is also visible on the hull side. Notice the track pin protruding from one of the links.

Another view of "211", this time being used as a photo prop. Notice how bright the white metal death's head collar emblems are on the tanker's black jacket, even in this blurry photo. The Tiger I was one of three from s.Pz.Abt.503 that suffered severe enough damage within the first month of combat in January 1943 that it was shipped back to Germany and subsequently retired to be used as a training tool at Paderborn, where these photos were taken. Notice the presence of left over whitewash on the hull front and the remnants of the toggle bolts beside the missing ball mount, used to secure the sealing cap for submerged fording. The complete Nebelwurfgerät assembly on the right side of the turret has been removed, but the welds for the bottom leg of the bracket are still visible. There appears to be a shell penetration indicated with white markings just below the turret lifting lug, as well as a deep gouge on the upper turret edge, both of which invariably helped lead to this Tiger's demise.

Many early Tigers soldiered on for quite some time like this vehicle with turret number "112" in black with white outline, painted in the distinctive style of 1.Kp./s.Pz.Abt.503, seen in the late summer or autumn of 1943 and finished in a three-color camouflage. It has the early track guards with bend in the middle and no triangular reinforcement plates as well as the turret Nebelwurfgerät but lacks the fasteners on the glacis for the long-handled shovel and S-mines. Other photos confirm it did not have the rear turret escape hatch, so all this points to a late October/November 1942 production date. Unusually, it appears that the twin openings for the driver's K.F.F.2 periscopes have been welded shut, the elimination of which did not occur until February 1943. Also clearly seen is the Pz.Kpfw.III turret stowage bin, used as an expedient solution until the standard production bin was introduced in late January 1943. The upturned track guard is for securing a roll of camouflage net as seen on other Tigers in this unit and notice the open cooling air grille with its mesh debris screen leaning against a road wheel.

Péter Kocsis

This is another s.Pz.Abt.503 Tiger I, most likely "122" from the 1st company with their uniquely shaped "2". It is a later production vehicle built between February and May 1943, since it has the mounting brackets to the left of the tow hitch for the engine starter crank handle but also the early single hole Schwungkraftanlasser (inertia hand-cranked starter) guide plate mounted between the exhausts, indicating that it still has a Maybach HL 210 P45 engine, replaced with the HL 230 P45 at Fgst. Nr.250251 in mid-May. The straight track guards are visible here, although the rearmost one appears to be one of the middle sections that has been relocated, given the shape of the triangular stiffener plate. S.Pz.Abt.503 removed the Fiefel filters from most, if not all, of their tanks but the mounting lugs can still be seen. Among the many missing parts are the round cover plates over the exhausts along with the sheet metal shrouds, and the cover plate over the left-hand idler adjustment port for tensioning the track. The photo was taken in the autumn of 1943, most likely in the Krasnograd – Kremenchug area of Ukraine.

Recovery was a constant problem for the schwere.Panzer-Abteilungen due to the lack of suitable recovery vehicles, as these whitewashed Tigers from 3.Kp./s.Pz.Abt.503 demonstrate attempting to pull "311" out of an icy, watery ditch in January 1944 around Vinnytsia in central Ukraine. This attempt ultimately failed, and it was not recovered for another few days. The four Tigers involved are, from back to front, "333", "312", "314" and an unknown numbered vehicle. In the background three more Tigers provide security. All of these Tigers were delivered to the battalion on 3 January 1944 and have the new turret with cast cupola, Zimmerit and a single headlight mounted in the middle of the front plate. Also visible on some are the external travel lock on the hull rear and Gleitschutzpickeln (metal chevrons) on the tracks, so production dates would have been between August and December 1943. 311 has a deep gouge from a shell strike on the upper edge of the turret above the number and also has damage to the second outer road wheel that undoubtedly caused it to lose its rubber tire.

The Archive of Modern Conflict

In mid-January 1944, Oberstleutnant Dr. Franz Bake, commander of Panzer-Regiment.11/6.Panzer-Division, was ordered to assemble schwere.Panzer-Regiment "Bake", to which 34 Tigers of s.Pz.Abt.503 were assigned. The ad hoc unit was used to counterattack the Russians east of Vinnytsia and relieve the German forces trapped in the Tscherkassy pocket. This Tiger I with solid black turret number "323" and worn whitewash has been identified as belonging to this unit and could be one of the 21 Tigers undergoing repairs in Potash, Ukraine that were captured by the Russians on 30 March 1944. The vehicle exhibits all the features seen on those in the previous photo and the tactical number and Balkenkreuz are consistent with the markings of 3.Kp./s.Pz.Abt.503.

Despite only a small portion of this Tiger I being visible, the track guards clearly show the bend following the edge of the hull, indicating it was built in November/early December 1942. The mounting lugs for the Feifel air filters are present as well, but the filters themselves have been removed. Above the mounting frame for the rear mudflap is the remnants of the track tool stowage box bracket, undoubtedly suffering damage along with the mudflap. The crewman in the foreground seems to be wearing a custom-tailored jacket in SS plane tree pattern, presumably made from a piece of zeltbahn (shelter quarter) given the central seam down the back. But the visible turret numbers on the Tiger are black with a white outline, which was not used by any of the SS heavy panzer companies. Given the upturned track guard, this could be another Tiger from s.Pz.Abt.503, which was attached to SS-Panzer-Grenadier-Division "Das Reich" in August 1943. It seems to be finished in three-color camouflage.

This whitewashed Tiger I is one of those abandoned in March 1944 during the retreat in the Tarnopol (now Ternopil) area of western Ukraine. It belonged to 13.Kp./SS-Panzer-Regiment 1, although that unit had been disbanded on March 1 and was in the process of transferring to Belgium to be re-built. The unexpected delivery of six new Tigers on March 5, of which the vehicle here is most likely one, meant integration into Panzergruppe SS-Pz.Div."LSSAH" and becoming part of Kampgruppe Kuhlmann until the middle of April. The Zimmerit, chevrons on the tracks, lack of S-Mine dischargers and rubber-tired road wheels indicate it was built between mid-October 1943 and January 1944. The spare tracks are uniquely held in place using two bent track pins welded to the front plate. It appears that one of the binocular sight holes in the mantlet has been plugged, even thought the monocular sight wasn't introduced until April 1944. Notice the damaged muzzle brake and missing road wheel from the first station, perhaps removed on purpose to stop the buildup of mud as was seen on many Tigers.

Péter Kocsis

The width of the Tiger I meant that, in order to transport it by rail, the track guards and eight outer road wheels had to be removed, and the Kgs 63/725/130 Marchketten (725 mm wide operational tracks) had to be replaced with Kgs 63/520/130 Verladeketten (520 mm wide transport tracks) as seen here. Below the cupola on the turret side is a Fgst. Nr. which appears to be "250325", indicating June 1943 production, even though records mention the new turret with cast cupola was only introduced in July 1943 with "250391". The Tiger looks in new condition, with a good view of the three S-Mine dischargers and early stowage pattern for the track changing cable that was modified in August 1943.

This late model Tiger I shows how they were typically loaded for rail transport, with the Marchketten stored underneath the vehicle. Assuming there was a loading ramp, the Marchketten could be loaded and unloaded by the Tiger itself by pulling the tracks with its tow cables, which is perhaps why one of the cables is laying at the front of the rail car. The single hole in the mantlet for the T.Z.F.9c monocular gun sight indicates it was built between April and August 1944 when production ended. The "Gummigefederten Stahllaufrollen" (rubber cushioned steel-tired road wheels) were introduced in February 1944 and one road wheel from each axle was eliminated (two per axle instead of three) which meant it was no longer necessary to remove the outer wheels for rail transport. Also visible here is the later stowage pattern of the track changing cable. Sitting on the glacis plate is a WR1/T entertainment receiver with its integral speaker that was issued by the Wehrmacht and which was capable of picking up radio stations on virtually any band, as well as being able to connect to gramophones and the like. Nicknamed "Rudi" and intended for frontline use, it was designed in 1940 by Blaupunkt, a brand name that is still in use today, and who is credited with developing the first FM car radio in 1949.

Péter Kocsis

After fighting in Tunisia and Sicily, s.Pz.Abt.504 was reestablishing in early 1944 and transferred to Italy in June. 3.Kompanie was the former Panzer-Kompanie 314 (Funklenk) used to operate the radio-controlled Borgward B IV explosive charge carrier, and its Tigers were equipped with the radio transmitter and had an additional antenna mount on the right side of the turret, not visible in this view of "334" being used for a photo opportunity. All the tanks were delivered in March and April so exhibited most of the late features like steel-tired road wheels but most still had the T.Z.F.9b binocular gun sight with the two holes in the mantlet. s.Pz.Abt.504 used a unique numbering style, with the first digit twice as large as the other two, painted in white with a black outline. The tanks were finished in a standard three-color camouflage of RAL 7028 Dunkelgelb, RAL 6003 Olivgrün and RAL 8017 Rotbraun. The bent track guard provides a view of the seldom seen triangular stiffeners on the underside and clearly shows the Zimmerit extended right to the bottom edge of the upper hull. 334 was commanded by an Unteroffizier (corporal) named Schmidt and abandoned during the retreat in late June 1944, between Pomarance and Saline in Tuscany.

This Tiger I from s.Pz.Abt.508 is pictured on 3 July 1944 in Cecina, Italy, south of Livorno, being examined by two medics from the U.S. 34th Infantry Division “Red Bull”, their unit patch visible above the Red Cross armband. It was lost during an attack on July 1 while supporting the 16.SS-Panzer-Grenadier-Division “Reichsführer-SS”, taking a hit on the right side into the engine compartment from a 75mm round fired by a U.S. Sherman from B Company of 752nd Tank Battalion. The puncture is just visible here where the smaller patch of Zimmerit is missing, which caused the fuel tank to ignite and start a fire. Two additional hits in the lower hull damaged the track, and given the buckled roof plate and gun in full recoil, a small internal explosion invariably occurred. Although not visible here, this Tiger wore tactical number "221". The difference between the Zimmerit patterns on the hull and mantlet compared to the turret is quite striking. On the ground between the two soldiers are a C-hook and the cover plate for the Bosch headlight.

This is another Tiger I from s.Pz.Abt.508, displaying the unusual numbering system they used, a single digit to designate the company. In this case, a "1" for 1.Kompanie, in white outline. Also visible is a worn Balkenkreuz above the motorcycle rider's head, in black with white outline that extends below the line of the track guard, indicating that the track guards were probably removed permanently. The open engine hatch suggests a breakdown that brought the Tiger to a sudden stop before having to be abandoned, and the very taut track seems to be a further indication of this. The turret ring guard is present, but the vehicle still has the binocular gun sight, so was built in February or March 1944. Notice the shell standing on the roof, presumably an 8.8cm Panzergranate Patrone 39 with its white-tipped blunt nose, the standard APCBC (Armor Piercing, Capped, Ballistic Cap) round for the Tiger.

Schwere Panzer-Kompanie Hummel was formed in the summer of 1944 using an ad hoc mix of fourteen Tigers taken from a training unit, Panzer-Ersatz und Ausbildungs-Abteilung 500, commanded by Hamptmann Hans Hummel. It was transferred to the Arnhem area in September to help counter Operation Market Garden. This early Tiger I complete with original drum cupola, turret number "131" in solid black, was lost during its employment in Holland and is being used for a photo by a British soldier. Given that it has the spare track link holders on the turret but lacks the loader's periscope, it was built in April-May 1943. The spare set of Tiger tracks looks to be a permanent addition as extra armor given that the securing rod is mounted through the track teeth. The three spare tracks between the ball mount and driver's vision port are the 520mm wide Verladeketten (transport tracks) with their distinctive round pin pockets on the ends. In the foreground are the remains of two British Universal Carriers.

This late production Tiger I from schwere SS-Panzer-Abteilung 102, formed in the spring of 1944, was lost during the two short months of combat and retreat through France in July and August 1944 that virtually wiped out the entire unit before they were sent for re-fitting with the Tiger II. The "blitzrune" lighting bolt unit insignia with a line underneath it is visible on the rear plate, typically painted in pink but possibly white here. Remnants of a turret number in white outline are also visible on the portions of Zimmerit still intact. Tigers of this unit were camouflaged with wide wavy bands of both RAL 6003 Olivgrün and RAL 8017 Rotbraun, leaving very little of the RAL 7028 Dunkelgelb visible. This vehicle has the lightweight muzzle brake that was designed for the Tiger II's 8.8cm Kw.K.43 L/71 but also installed on the Tiger I starting in April 1944. It is also equipped with the T.Z.F.9c monocular gun sight but still lacks the Pilzen (sockets) on the turret roof for the 2-ton jib boom that were introduced in June. Throughout the Tiger's production period the loader's hatch had numerous variations including both welded and press-formed versions, and the final version is seen here.

3. GEPANZERTER ZUGKRAFTWAGEN & 8.8CM FLAK 18 „BUNKERKNACKER"

The Archive of Modern Conflict

In August 1938 an order was issued for the development of a modified 8.8cm Flak 18 and armored towing tractor to be used for combating fortifications. This combination has been colloquially referred to as "BunkerFlak"," BunkerPak" and most commonly, "Bunkerknacker" (bunker buster). In two short months production had already started and the initial vehicles were used during the occupation of the Sudetenland in October 1938 as seen here, with this column moving through Märisch-Schönberg (today known as Šumperk, Czech Republic) under a banner welcoming the liberation. The gun is painted in the "Buntfarbenanstrich" scheme (literally colorful pattern or paint) of Erdgelb No.17 (Earth Yellow), Braun No.18 (Brown) and Grün No.28 (Green), which is unusual since this was discontinued in July 1937 before these guns were built. The gepanzerte 8t Zugkraftwagen (armored 8-ton tractor) would appear to be painted in the 1937 camouflage of 2/3 Dunkelgrau No.46 (Dark Grey) and 1/3 Dunkelbraun No.45 (Dark Brown).

The gepanzerte Zugkraftwagen was built using a KM m 11 Sd.Kfz.7 chassis supplied by Kraus-Maffei, to which Weserhütte AG manufactured and mounted 15mm armored structures around the engine and crew compartments. The superstructure vaguely resembled that of the Sd.Kfz.251 and had an armored cab for the driver and commander, accommodation for six men in an open topped area behind that, and a magazine at the back of the vehicle with rear opening doors for 24 rounds of 8.8cm ammunition. It is unknown how many vehicles were converted, but license plates document at least 25 different vehicles. The solid white squares on "WH-291262" are an unknown marking that appear on a couple of these vehicles and could be associated with schwere Panzer-Jäger-Abteilung 605 (s.Pz.Jg.Abt.605), one of three units equipped with the Bunkerknacker. Prior to the start of the war, colored geometric symbols were one of the methods for designating a platoon(zug), white typically being associated with 1.Zug. Both the vehicle and gun are finished in Dunkelgrau No.46 and Dunkelbraun No.45. Notice the folded side shields on the Flak 18.

This photo provides a good view of the modifications made to the Flak 18 mounted on its Sonderanhänger 201 (Sd.Ah.201 / Special Trailer 201) to make it suitable for attacking bunkers. The gun was meant to be brought into action quickly and fired from its carriage. Along with the modified shield with folding sides, the fuse setter on the left side of the gun was replaced with a ready ammunition bin with six 8.8cm rounds and a small platform for the loader to stand on, visible here. On the opposite side, the elevation and traverse controls were modified so that one gunner could control both, unlike the standard gun that required two crewmen. The Lafettenkreuz 18 (cross-shaped carriage) had the two side legs shortened and strengthened, with larger feet and a quick release mechanism via a foot control. The legs are in a partially lowered position in this photo. Notice the bright bare metal of the breechblock and how visible the Dunkelgrau No.46 and Dunkelbraun No.45 camouflage is on both guns and Zugkraftwagen. A white rectangle has been painted on the fender of the halftrack, but no registration number has been applied.

A Bunkerknacker is seen in action during the French campaign in May-June 1940, with another gun's barrel just visible in the background. The loader is manning his position, having removed a round from the ready bin and is just about to push it into the breech. The side outriggers have been fully deployed and were meant to stabilize the gun when firing over the side. Note that the gun is being pulled by a standard Sd.Kfz.7 8-ton halftrack. Rheinmetall documented production of 50 guns but since it is unknown how many gepanzerte Zugkraftwagen were produced, there may not have been enough to go around, and units were forced to use unarmored vehicles to make up the excess. Just visible below the license plate "WH-27714" is a white tactical symbol for a motorized heavy anti-tank battalion (schwere panzer-jäger-abteilung).

The tow cable attached to the front towing pintle of this gepanzerte Zugkraftwagen could explain the open hood and apparent engine repairs. Visible on the right fender of "WH-311056" is the insignia of s.Pz.Jg.Abt.525. The colored rectangle is probably in yellow, as is the first part of the text below, followed by "525" in white. The color could indicate the company, whereas the unreadable first two digits separated by a forward slash could indicate platoon (Zug) and section. On the left fender is a white "19" possibly indicating the individual halftrack number within the entire battalion. It is presumed that the three Abteilungen equipped with Bunkerknacker were organized according to Kriegsstärkenachweisung 1145 (K.St.N. / table of organization) dated February 1, 1940, which meant they were equipped with 15 gepanzerte Zugkraftwagen/Sd.Kfz.7 and 21 Sd.Kfz.10 1-ton halftracks, so this could be a vehicle in 2.Kompanie, which would match with the colored rectangle since yellow was the commonly used color for a 2nd company. At the rear of the left fender two wheel chocks are stowed. Notice that the interior is painted RAL 1001 Elfenbein (Ivory) as seen on the open vision ports.

Péter Kocsis

The third unit to be equipped with the Bunkerknacker was s.Pz.Jg.Abt.560. Their white insignia on the fender of this gepanzerte Zugkraftwagen clearly states "Pz.- Abt.560" in an unusual font, below the tactical symbol for a towed anti-tank gun company with the company number beside it, in this case "3" for 3.Kompanie. A tow cable is wrapped around the brackets between the two forward armor plates and one of the engine compartment side access panels has been removed and is sitting behind the headlight. The interior of this vehicle's vision ports appear to be painted Dunkelgrau No.46, whose designation changed to RAL 7021 Dunkelgrau when the new 4-digit RAL system was introduced in 1940. To the right of "WH-311238" is its associated Flak 18.

This would appear to be the same vehicle seen in the previous photo, as the last three digits of the license plate ("238") can just be made out through the foliage and the "WH" is in the same thin font. The overhead canopy makes this gepanzerte Zugkraftwagen appear to be heavily camouflaged, but it would still be finished in 2/3 Dunkelgrau No.46 (Dark Grey) and 1/3 Dunkelbraun No.45 (Dark Brown). On the left fender is white "27", once again possibly representing the individual vehicle in the entire battalion, in this case one from 3.Kompanie that corresponds with the "3" on the tactical symbol. Notice that the vehicle's roof tarpaulin is in place. An access hatch was installed on each side of the driver's compartment but does not seem to have been used very often. Two rubber stoppers are visible on the top edge to keep it from banging on the fender. Stowed on the fender is a long crowbar, engine starting crank, jack block and 5-ton jack.

With its gunner and loader already in position and the travel lock disengaged, this Bunkerknacker appears to be moving up to provide covering fire for the unit to the right that has taken cover on the roadside during the French campaign. Barely visible in the bright sunlight is the s.Pz.Jg.Abt.560 insignia on the right door of the ammunition bin on the rear of the gepanzerte Zugkraftwagen. The spare tire attached to the rear bogie of the Sd.Ah.201 trailer was also characteristic of this unit. Also on the rear bogie are two of the three-round wicker containers with metal end caps and wooden corners that the 8.8cm shells were shipped in. Another one is visible on top of the Zugkraftwagen's ammo bin. The crew compartment roof tarpaulin is folded back, and the vehicle's engine hood appears to be laying on the front bogie of the Sd.Ah.201.

While an officer and two unteroffiziere (non-commissioned officers) confer on a French roadside, a Bunkerknacker from s.Pz.Jg.Abt.560 passes by, displaying the unit insignia on the rear ammunition bin of the gepanzerte Zugkraftwagen and the characteristic spare tire mount on the rear of the Sd.Ah.201. It also carries the vehicle number "16" in white, presumably indicating it is from 2.Kompanie. The open rear door and erected roof tarpaulin provide a unique view showing that the tarpaulin had a corresponding opening in it as well. The driver's side vision flap is fully open too. The crew has covered the gun breech and ready ammo bin to keep the dust out and a gun-in-battery letter white "C" can be seen on the inside of the 10mm thick gun shield. The car on the right is a BMW 326 four-seat cabriolet while on the left is an Adler 2.5 liter Type 10 cabriolet, the so called "Autobahn Adler".

No markings are visible on this Bunkerflak but the rear bogie of the Sd.Ah.201 trailer has the typical spare tire bracket, so it is presumably from s.Pz.Jg.Abt.560. The bright metal unpainted finish of the end of the breech block and the elevation quadrant that indicated elevation during direct firing is quite prominent. A number of Bunkerflak were seen carrying large spools of cable or wire and the fitting on the front of the trailer was used for that, appearing empty here. The crew seems ready for action and are just waiting for the order to move forward. They could also be waiting on resupply given the open rear magazine doors.

The complete eight-man crew of a Bunkerflak poses for a picture on their gepanzerte Zugkraftwagen, complete with two 8.8cm shells and a bottle of wine. Perhaps they are about to christen their new vehicle named "Brecher", which means "to break" or "to shatter" in German, most appropriate for a bunker buster. Notice two double quotation marks to the bottom left and top right of the name! Visible on the left fender is what appears to be the tactical symbol for a towed anti-tank gun company and next to the hull door is a scrawled number "16061", which could be a chassis number and falls within the range produced by Krauss-Maffei, the supplier of the Zugkraftwagen chassis. The gun commander, most likely an unteroffiziere, is standing the highest and below him holding the shell is a gefreiter (lance corporal) with the typical chevron on his arm. In the left background is a standard Sd.Kfz.7 halftrack with its canvas top erected complete with side panels and covers over the door openings.

Once again, the white tactical symbol for a towed anti-tank gun company can be seen on the left fender of this gepanzerte Zugkraftwagen , but this time it resembles a style that might be attributed to s.Pz.Jg.Abt.605. The gun commander appears to be conferring with his superior, undoubtedly the owner of the staff car in the foreground. The crew lounges around on the armored ammunition bin waiting for orders. On the fender is the three-round wicker shell container, which seems to be mounted in a poor spot given that it blocks the opening of the hull door. The feeble attempt at foliage camouflage on the front is almost comical. Notice the lanyard attached to the muzzle cover, presumably tied such that the cover will be pulled off by itself as soon as the gun goes into action.

Péter Kocsis

This thoroughly wrecked Bunkerflak was destroyed in Valenciennes, France so presumably belonged to s.Pz.Jg.Abt.605, as this was the only one of the three units equipped with Bunkerflak attached to IV.Armeekorps of Heeresgruppe B, and this area was part of their section of the front during Operation Fall Gelb (Case Yellow), the invasion of France and the low countries. The gepanzerte Zugkraftwagen is completely burned out, with no rubber left on any of the wheels and the paint quite scorched, indicating a very intense fire. The engine hood is laying on the ground in front of it and curiously enough there appears to be an MG 13 on the ground beside the sidewalk.

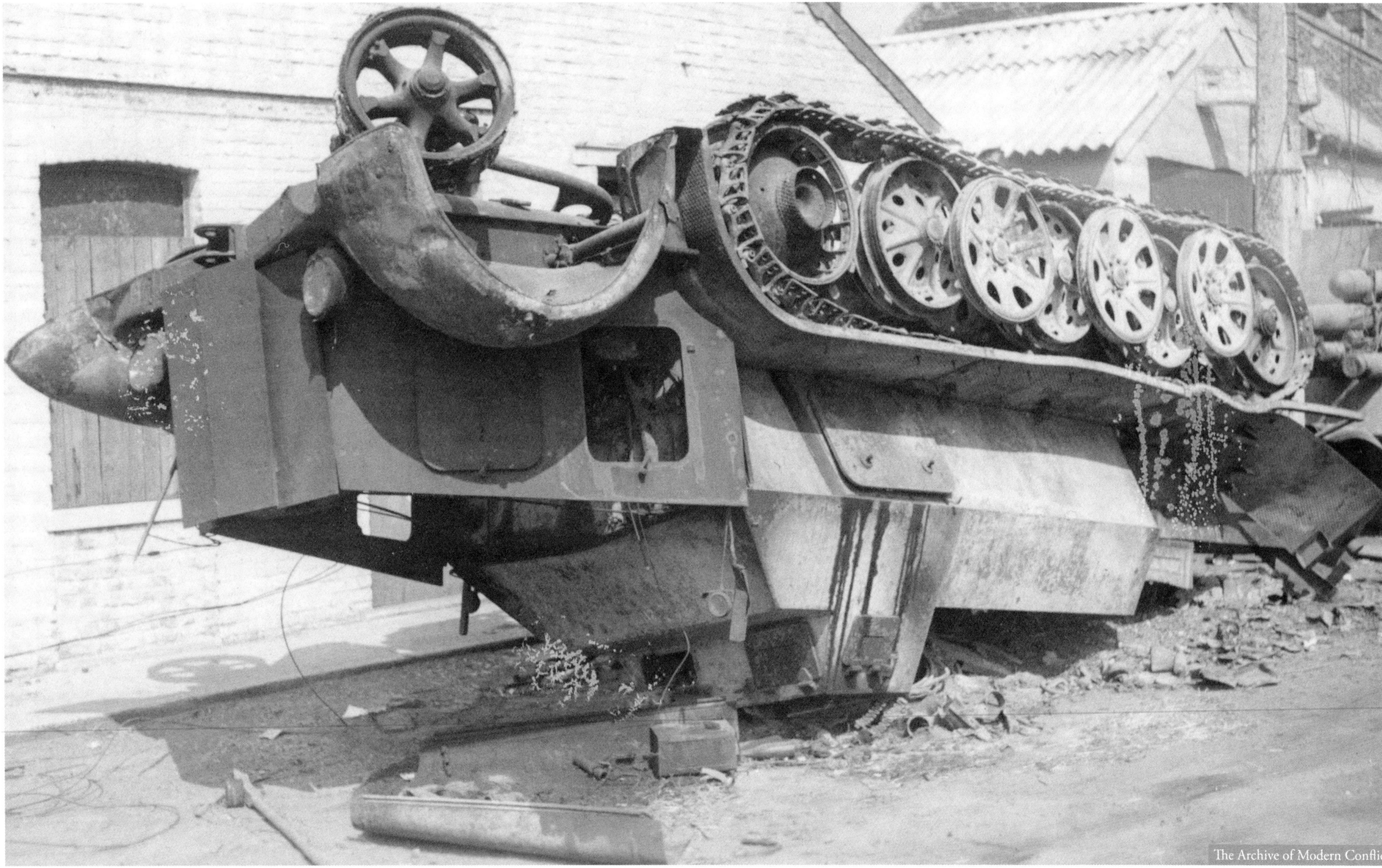

This closeup photo of the gepanzerte Zugkraftwagen seems to have been taken before the previous one as the side hatch is closed and there is a long crowbar on the ground in front of the hood, so presumably scavengers came by afterwards and looked inside for useful materials before taking the crowbar. Notice that the rubber bump stops have also burned off of the side hatch. Unfortunately, the only visible markings are the last two digits of the license plate, "15". The triangular tubular support for the front axle that helped absorb forces in the driving direction is visible by the front wheel.

A rear view shows that even the rubber track pads have burned off. Given the state of the ammunition bin, it would appear that this may have exploded. The tow coupling as well as the rollers and cable for the frame mounted winch are visible here. One of the wheel chocks normally stowed on the right-hand side fender is visible at the right edge of the photo. The positioning of both halftrack and Flak 18 in relation to the concrete power pole suggests that they were probably pushed to the side of the road, the vehicle rolling over in the process and spilling its flame damaged debris.

A closeup picture of the damaged Flak 18, which only suffered fire damage to the front. Notice the specific location on the barrel for the travel lock, with raised ridges around its circumference for securing the bicycle style chain, which is hanging on the far side. The maintenance hatch is open on the cruciform mount, a rarely seen detail. The two steel plates in the foreground appear to be the armored doors of the gepanzerte Zugkraftwagen's rear ammunition bin. All manner of detritus is scattered around including one of the wheel chocks, gas mask canister, and a 5-ton jack.

The Archive of Modern Conflict

Given that all three schwere Panzer-Jäger-Abteilungen equipped with Bunkerflak were converted back to standard units with towed 3.7 cm Pak after the French campaign, this picture was invariably taken in France during the winter of 1940-41 given the snowy conditions. The gepanzerte Zugkraftwagen is once again completely burned out, missing all the rubber from the front wheels, road wheels and track pads. The left side portion of the rear ammunition bin is missing, providing a clear view of the rear crew door. The chains visible under the front of the vehicle suggest that a recovery attempt must have been made at some point. In the left background is a typical water well with the bucket hanging from the top crossbeam.

Péter Kocsis

Activity up the hill has caught the attention of everyone on this road, included the crew of a Bunkerflak stopped behind a Kfz.70 Krupp Protze L 2 H 43/H 143 6x4 truck. The front bogie of the Flak 18 is missing its fenders. On the fender of the gepanzerte Zugkraftwagen are two three-round wicker shell containers and one of the removable panels from the armored side of the engine compartment. The foliage on the gun was probably useful to break up its outline when the Zugkraftwagen pulled or backed it into position amongst a treeline.

This profile view of a gepanzerte Zugkraftwagen shows the two-color camouflage of 2/3 Dunkelgrau No.46 and 1/3 Dunkelbraun No.45. It is not documented as to why the Bunkerflak units reverted back to standard 3.7 cm anti-tank guns, or what happened to the remaining Bunkerflak equipment after the French campaign, but presumably their tactical mobility left them exposed to attack while trying to position the Flak 18. An infantry unit takes a break in the foreground next to a railway switch.

Individual vehicle markings were a rarity on gepanzerte Zugkraftwagen so the stylized skull and crossbones, or Totenkopf, along with a swastika is quite unique. Two engine access panels have been removed on "WH-291014" and are laying against the damaged fenders. As noted in a previous photo, the dark square seen on the left fender could mean that this vehicle is from s.Pz.Jg.Abt.605 and the color, possibly red or black, indicated the platoon. Just visible on the side, as well as on the side of the gepanzerte Zugkraftwagen to the left, are narrow white outline Balkenkreuz, another marking that was seldom seen on these vehicles.

4. 15 CM S.I.G.33 (SF) AUF PZ.KPFW.I AUSF.B

Péter Kocsis

While an effective infantry support weapon, the relatively short range and excessive weight of the 15 cm schwere Infanteriegeschütz 33 (s.I.G.33) resulted in a desire to make it more mobile. The 15 cm s.I.G.33 (Sf) auf Pz.Kpfw.I Ausf.B was the first such attempt, a very makeshift solution that mounted the entire gun including its wheels and shield on a very overstressed Pz.Kpfw.I chassis with a simple 10 mm thick 3-sided armored superstructure. Six companies of six guns each were in place at the start of Fall Gelb in May 1940, including s.IG.-Kompanie (mot.S) 701 to which the vehicle seen here was attached to. As was typical for artillery units, vehicles were marked with gun-in-battery letters, usually on the cover over the gun's wheel hub, in this case "C" in white. Of the six units in this campaign, s.IG. Kp.(mot.S) 701 was the only one to have the Balkenkreuz below the wheel hub cover, in black with a white outline. In the foreground is a typical 1940s French Yield sign, presumably made of white painted concrete, in yellow with a dark blue outline.

S.IG.Kp.(mot.S) 701 was also one of the three units that took part in the Balkans campaign and Unternehmen Marita (Operation Marita), the German invasion of Greece in April 1941. It was once again attached to 9.Panzer-Division, as it was during Fall Gelb, although in this photo of gun "A" loaded onto a Sd.Ah.115 trailer taken before the start of the campaign it did not yet have the divisional insignia applied as seen later on. Between the two campaigns the guns were repainted from the two-color camouflage of 2/3 Dunkelgrau No.46 and 1/3 Dunkelbraun No.45 to solid RAL 7021 Dunkelgrau as per the July 1940 order, which explains why the markings changed. The Balkenkreuz was now above the wheel hub cover and the distinctly block letter style of "A" replaced the standard shaped "A" seen in France. On the far side is a white tactical symbol for a self-propelled heavy gun company. The tarpaulin frame at the rear was added to a number of vehicles after Fall Gelb, and the heavy bar beside the engine compartment was a reinforcement strip due to the weight of the gun.

All six s.IG.Kp.(mot.S) took part in Operation Barbarossa in June 1941, still fully equipped with six guns each. While no markings are visible on this foliage covered 15 cm s.I.G.33 (Sf) auf Pz.Kpfw.I Ausf.B other then hints of a tactical marking on the right side, only s.IG.Kp.(mot.S) 701 was known to carry two spare road wheels on the front of the superstructure as seen here, added prior to the start of the campaign. Another spare road wheel lays on top of spare track sections on the glacis plate. Given that the gun severely overstressed the chassis, track and road wheel failures were undoubtedly common. Surprisingly, the vehicle's front mudflaps are still fully intact. s.IG.Kp.(mot.S) 701 was again attached to 9.Panzer-Division for the invasion of Russia, remaining with them until being disbanded in 1942 after losing all of its guns.

Given the spare road wheel stowage, this very dusty 15 cm s.I.G.33 (Sf) auf Pz.Kpfw.I Ausf.B is also presumably from s.IG.Kp.(mot.S) 701. Other then the enlisted man to the left, all the other men with binoculars in hand apparently watching the fall of shot or an attack going in are non-commissioned officers including an Oberfeldwebel (master sergeant) closest to the camera. The small size of the gun is readily apparent here. The barrel's muzzle cover is hanging below it just above the right soldier's head.

During the French campaign, s.IG.Kp.(mot.S) 702 carried a unique white panzer rhomboid with a stylized tactical marking for a self-propelled heavy gun company superimposed and the number "702" below, making identification simple. Opposite that was the white oakleaf insignia of 1.Pz.Div. and "G" for Panzergruppe Guderian, to which this division was attached. Although barely visible, this is gun "F", the only one in the company to have the oak leaf on the sloped armor; all other five guns had both markings on the flat front plate. Notice the muzzle cover hanging below the barrel. The large mix of markings seen on the surrounding vehicles is quite interesting, with the "G" painted slightly different on all of them. Given the French Citroen 11CV Traction Avant in front, the picture was probably taken during Fall Rot (Case Red) in June 1940. The tactical symbol is for the 3rd battery of a towed artillery battalion, also seen on the Einheits-Diesel and other trucks following the 15 cm s.I.G.33 (Sf) auf Pz.Kpfw.I Ausf.B. To the left is an Sd.Kfz.223 with a pennant insignia denoting attachment to a headquarters, and following it is an Sd.Kfz.10 1-ton halftrack with a motorized infantry tactical sign. All vehicles carry the 1.Pz.Div. oakleaf.

Although the white picket fence might suggest otherwise, this is gun "E" from s.IG.Kp.(mot.S) 702 during Operation Barbarossa. The unit was still attached to 1.Pz.Div., which changed their divisional insignia to an inverted yellow "Y" as seen here above the proper tactical insignia in white for a self-propelled heavy gun company. The same markings are repeated on the side below the wheel hub cover plate. The Balkenkreuz is in white outline only. The crew has undoubtedly learned from experience that the overloaded chassis was hard on the suspension and has stockpiled numerous spare track sections on the glacis. Notice how bright the road wheel rims appear from constant wear by the track teeth. Following behind is an Sd.Kfz.10 halftrack, most likely one of the ammunition vehicles.

Péter Kocsis

For the Russian campaign, s.IG.Kp.(mot.S) 702 utilized unique stowage for spare road wheels, with one mounted on the rear plate as seen in the French campaign, but another mounted on the s.I.G.33 gun trail. On top of this was a spare return roller. Visible here are the two vertical stiffening bars added to the rear plate to help stabilize the engine deck when the gun was fired, given that the gun trail was attached to it. All manner of other stowage is visible including canteens, mess kits and a map case, and the NCO sitting on the gun trail, presumably the gun commander, has four M1924 Steilhandgranate (stick hand grenades) stuck in his belt.

S.IG.Kp.(mot.S) 702 continued to soldier on during the winter of 1941/42. Gun "E" is seen here once again, now with a scruffy whitewash coat applied neatly around the Balkenkreuz leaving a very thin outline of RAL 7021 Dunkelgrau. The vehicle has been parked on small logs to keep from sinking into the soft ground during firing, and a large panel, presumably wood, has been placed against the front superstructure, undoubtedly for extra armor protection. Behind the gun, also positioned on logs to keep them dry, is a stack of s.I.G.33 shells still in their woven wicker transport containers, and boxes of charges. The spare road wheel on the gun trail is stowed differently here, at an angle, and on the rear fender is what appears to be a French heavy jack, sometimes seen on FT-17s and probably salvaged during the unit's service in the French campaign. In the right background is another gun, also with a tarpaulin covering virtually the entire open top and rear.

Four of the six s.IG. Kompanies named their guns, using a name starting with the gun-in-battery letter for each vehicle. During the French campaign, s.IG.Kp.(mot.S) 703 used the name "Edith" for gun "E", painted in a white Gothic-style script below the gun barrel. The white gun-in-battery letter E is visible on the wheel hub cover. The transmission access hatch has been removed, which was commonly seen on 15 cm s.I.G.33 (Sf) auf Pz.Kpfw.I Ausf.B, perhaps due to constant overheating because of the overstressed chassis. To the right is a BMW R-12 motorcycle, still with a civilian style front fender, the BMW badge quite prominent on the side of the frame. On the sidecar is a Red Cross marking and the front fender has the tactical symbol for a motorcycle platoon. Following behind is a diesel Mercedes-Benz 6x4 LG 3000 3-ton truck.

"Edith" is seen here at a later date, after presumably suffering the loss of a crewman with the addition of an Iron Cross marking in black with a white outline on the internal gun shield of the s.I.G. 33 gun itself. A date of "29.5.40" is below the cross, only partially visible here. The drive sprocket has been removed which provides a look at how it was attached to the drive axle. Notice that the left front tow hook has been bent upward vertically and the right one appears to be missing. A French Adrian helmet is on the glacis. The Einheits-Diesel truck parked behind the gun has a tactical symbol for a towed anti-tank gun company on its fender.

Three of the six units equipped with 15 cm s.I.G.33 (Sf) auf Pz.Kpfw.I Ausf.B took part in the Balkans campaign, including s.IG.Kp.(mot.S) 703. Like all the units, their guns were repainted in solid RAL 7021 Dunkelgrau after the French campaign and the markings reapplied. The names were repainted in white in the same position but using a block style script as seen on "Bismarck", gun "B". The Balkenkreuz was now painted below the wheel hub cover, in black with a white outline. Beside the standard white tactical symbol on the front is the yellow divisional insignia of an inverted "Y" with tick mark used by 2.Pz.Div. beginning in 1940. All guns in the company also had wire mesh attached to the front and sides for this campaign, presumably to attach foliage, but none appears in any photographs. The mesh meant that the front sight door could no longer be opened and the Zieleinrichtung 34 (Aiming Device 34) not used but based on photographs it seems like this was seldom used anyways. Instead, the Rundblickfernrohr 32 (Rbl.F.32 / Panoramic Telescope 32) was used for targeting, mounted on an extension that allowed it to see over the top of the superstructure. Notice the erected tarpaulin frame at the rear.

The size and shape of the gun-in-battery letter "D" and the location and style of Balkenkreuz markings indicate that this vehicle is probably from s.IG.Kp.(mot.S) 704. The picture was taken during the French campaign given the buildings in the background and crewman still wearing the M1934 Schutzmütze (padded beret). Notice that the gun-in-battery letter D is also repeated on the inside of the left door below the firing tables. Given the shortage of ammunition stowage space, it was common practice to store two additional shells vertically in the opening of the gun trail, to complement the other four carried – two on the left fender, one on the right and one on the engine deck directly under the aforementioned opening visible here, although in this case it has been removed from its wicker container. Both Balkenkreuz are painted in white outline only.

The fragile nature of the overloaded chassis of the 15 cm s.I.G.33 (Sf) auf Pz.Kpfw.I Ausf.B meant that it was always preferable to haul the guns over long distances, such as gun "F" seen here from s.IG. Kp.(mot.S) 704 loaded on a Sonderanhänger 115 (Sd.Ah.115) 10-ton transport trailer. Other then the missing front mudflap, the gun is in pristine condition and a good view is provided of the white letter and Balkenkreuz markings. At the rear of the gun trail is an unusual bracket, similar to ones seen on some other guns in this unit. Another picture of gun "F" at a later date suggests that these were used to hold vertical timbers, presumably to support a taller, larger tarpaulin cover.

This gun is undergoing training prior to the invasion of France. Other then the worn Balkenkreuz on the rear plate, another one can be seen on the superstructure side painted well above the wheel hub cover, which is indicative of s.IG.Kp.(mot.S) 705, which also used very small gun-in-battery letters. Clearly visible here is the Rundblickfernrohr 32 (Rbl.F.32) mounted on its extension. Of interest is the antenna socket mounted on the rear left corner of the engine deck, since radio equipment was not part of the standard equipment for the 15 cm s.I.G.33 (Sf) auf Pz.Kpfw.I Ausf.B, but some crews obviously adapted. Hanging off the rear is a purpose-made cover to protect the entire barrel assembly and visible in front of the right crewman stored in a bracket is a traffic paddle in red with a white outline, so it was presumably part of the gun's issued equipment.

This photo provides a clear view of the white outline Balkenkreuz on the side and the small gun-in-battery letters used by s.IG.Kp.(mot.S) 705, in this case gun "A". The unit also named their guns using this letter, so gun A was named "Anni". Of interest are the white markings on the glacis plate, which includes "705" to identify the unit and a five-digit Fahrgestell Nummer (Chassis Number) on the transmission access plate, starting with "14"; guns were converted from Pz.Kpfw.I Ausf.B chassis in the 10456-16500 range. An antenna socket is visible here in the same position as the previous picture, and two shells are stored in their brackets on the fender. Both the headlight and marker lights are missing their blackout covers, which is unusual. Following behind is one of the Sd.Kfz.10 ammunition vehicles.

The Sd.Ah.32 ammunition trailer on the left side of this picture is in fact being towed by the Sd.Kfz.10 seen in the previous photo. The rack between the stowage boxes holds four s.I.G.33 rounds in their wicker containers. Each gun was assigned two Sd.Kfz.10 and one Sd.Ah.32, so the second halftrack with license plate "WH-671217" is part of Anni's entourage, equipped with an MG 34 for anti-aircraft protection. Note the camouflaged cover over the windshield and a lucky horseshoe on the radiator screen. There is a "705" marking on the left fender, which seems to be on all the vehicles visible here. Following behind is gun "B", named "Berta". Although they are illegible, it too carries the "705" and Fahrgestell Nummer on the front glacis plate.

A clearer picture of "Berta" showing how small the gun-in-battery letters were as it is barely legible here. This gun also has an aerial mount in the same position as Anni and carries a full complement of ammunition, including the habitual two rounds stuffed through the gun trail opening and resting on the round secured to the engine deck. Behind this are charge boxes. The inside of the track teeth have been worn to bright metal rubbing against the road wheels. s.IG.Kp.(mot.S) 705 was attached to 7.Pz.Div. for Fall Gelb, as clearly indicated by the five Pz.Kpfw.38(t)s seen in the background, which was one of only two divisions equipped with this vehicle for this campaign. The large red numbers with white outline are also indicative of this division. Also seen are a Pz.Kpfw.II and Pz.Kpfw.IV. Note the Sd.Kfz.10 on the left with license plate number "WH-671214", only three vehicles removed from the one seen in the previous photo. It also has an antenna mount fixed to the top of the rear plate, so it would seem that this unit managed to equip itself with extensive radio equipment.

Unfortunately, the vegetation in the foreground is obscuring some of the wheel hub cover, however the fact that no portion of a gun-in-battery letter is visible along with the higher position of the Balkenkreuz and the presence of an antenna mount on the rear left side suggest this is a 15 cm s.I.G.33 (Sf) auf Pz.Kpfw.I Ausf.B from s.IG.Kp.(mot.S) 705 in the French campaign. While no antenna is mounted, the crewman on the left with his hand on the extension for the Rbl.F.32 sight is wearing headphones, so a radio is undoubtedly being carried. As was typical, two additional rounds are carried vertically and rest on the shell stowed on the engine deck, its end visible here.

s.IG.Kp.(mot.S) 706 was unique amongst the six companies in carrying the gun-in-battery letters on the left side of the front plate instead of the wheel hub covers on the side, in this case gun "A". There can be no disputing the unit, with white "706" on the right side of the front plate above the slanted yellow bar insignia of 10.Pz.Div. to which it was attached during the French campaign. Also seen is a small white "K", since this division was part of Panzergruppe von Kleist for both Fall Gelb and Fall Rot. On the recoil brake housing below the barrel is clearly seen the word "braun" in white, which was the fluid used in the recoil cylinder. Notice the missing transmission cover once again, no doubt to assist in keeping it from overheating. Behind the gun are three Sd.Kfz.10 halftracks from the ammunition sections, all carrying white gun-in-battery letters on their left fenders, "B" in the middle, "A" to the left and "F" in the background. They also have the other unit markings on the right fender. Under the tree is a captured British Morris Commercial CS8 already marked with "WH" on its front grille.

Gun “F” is also from s.IG.Kp.(mot.S) 706, but displays slightly different markings, with a larger “K” below the 10.Pz.Div. insignia. Of interest is the same yellow divisional marking repeated on the side door above the “K”, but in this case it has been incorrectly applied, with the slant of the line going in the opposite direction. The Balkenkreuz is black with a white outline, whereas gun “A” in the previous photo appeared to have only a white outline Balkenkreuz. The transmission cover is also missing and only one of the two shells is stowed on the rear fender. The photo was taken in Belgium during the early days of Fall Gelb.

Péter Kocsis

As the Wehrmacht became more and more adept at manoeuvre warfare, the need for self-propelled artillery in Panzer-Divisionen became apparent. For carrying the 15cm schwere Feldhaubitze 18 (s.F.H.18), the Geschützwagen III/IV für s.F.H.18/1 (Sf.) (Sd.Kfz.165) "Hummel" (Bumblebee) was the result, combining a slightly modified howitzer with a chassis consisting of Pz.Kpfw.III drive components (including sprockets) and Pz.Kpfw.IV motor and suspension. The vehicle seen here painted in three-color camouflage of RAL 7028 Dunkelgelb, RAL 6003 Olivgrün and RAL 8017 Rotbraun is one of the first 80 or so vehicles produced between February and May 1943, as it still mounts twin Bosch headlights, the right side one being dropped in late May. It also has Pz.Kpfw.IV Ausf.D idlers, another early feature. The rear mudflaps are similar to the Pz.Kpfw.IV and were not factory fitted, but instead backfitted by various units in the field. The open driver's vison port reveals its vision block housing, painted in RAL 1001 Elfenbein. To the right is a StuG III Ausf.G with tactical number white "302" on its side skirt, painted in a stencil pattern.

Another feature of early production Hummels was the exhaust muffler seen here on the nearest vehicle of a trainload of five vehicles that all appear to be brand new. This was eliminated from production in August 1943 after about 175 Hummels had been produced. Above the muffler is the prominently painted red and white striped ranging poles. The next two vehicles have twin headlights so are also early production vehicles, whereas the farthest two have rear mudflaps like the closest vehicle, although it has already lost its left one, perhaps while being loaded. The open rear doors provide a good view of the internal travel lock that engaged the gun cradle with two pins, the handle of one seen on the right side.

Péter Kocsis

Given the Peugeot 202 sedan sitting in front of it, this is the same Hummel seen in the previous photo. Both vehicles are finished in solid RAL 7028 Dunkelgelb with the only visible marking being the black and white Balkenkreuz on the side of the Hummel. Other then wooden chocks, it appears that only very small diameter cables have been used to secure it to the railcar. This view confirms that it also has the twin Bosch headlights. The "wicker" style mats hanging from the barrels are presumably for placing ammunition and charges on when stockpiling on the ground beside the Hummel for long fire missions, or perhaps for leaning against the vehicle to help breakup its outline while in position.

This Hummel is from the same unit seen loaded on railcars in the previous photos, now in a camouflaged fire position. This view shows that the idler wheel is the much more common welded tubular version first used on the Pz.Kpfw.IV Ausf.F. Notice that the spring-loaded rear mudflap has been flipped up, which does not allow the rear door to be fully opened. Prominently displayed on the side of the recoil brake housing below the barrel is a black placard with maintenance instructions, typically quite visible on most Hummels. The standard organization for the Panzer-Division's artillery regiment was to have one battalion, typically the I.Abteilung, outfitted as a self-propelled unit, with two batteries of six 10.5cm Sd.Kfz.124 "Wespe" (Wasp) and one battery (usually the 3rd) of six Hummels.

Péter Kocsis

While most Hummels used drive sprockets first introduced on the Pz.Kpfw.III Ausf.H, a select few had the earlier ones used on the Ausf.E to G, with its distinctive eight round holes, as seen on this vehicle. It also as the twin Bosch headlights and mudflaps at the rear, although the object on the glacis plate appears to be the mudflap from the right side. It is once again finished in solid RAL 7028 Dunkelgelb, with even the spare tracks on the lower front hull being painted. The bolts and plates for securing the spare tracks can be seen. Notice the identity disc (the German version of American "dog tags") hanging around the neck of the crewmember sitting on the fender.

This Hummel still has the exhaust muffler but lacks the right-side Bosch headlight so is one of the vehicles built between May and August 1943, production amounting to 129 in these four months out of a total production quantity of 705 between February 1943 and March 1945. Visible around the muffler is a tight-fitting sheet metal heat guard to keep the crew from burning themselves on the hot exhaust. The normal crew size was six, so this Hummel has gained an extra one. The pole sticking out from the front is most likely part of the gun cleaning rod, which many Hummel crews kept assembled and readily available. A spare road wheel is stored on the glacis and the dark spot on the barrel is worn paint from the travel lock.

This photo of another early production Hummel was taken in November 1943 and shows how the grain or wheat stalks seen in the previous picture could be used to break up the outline of the vehicle. This Hummel also has mudflaps at the rear and carries a spare road wheel on the front superstructure armor. It is interesting to note that the three-color camouflage extends to the inside of the rear doors. The white gun-in-battery letter "D" is presumably painted on the exterior of the door or rear wall as well so it would be visible during movement. Most of the crew and their "guests" are wearing M1942 padded reversible white/camouflage winter tunics and trousers, in either M1943 "marsh" or "splinter" patterns. The officer to the right is a bit unusually dressed – a M1943 field cap without the regulation aluminum wire piping and an M1942 reed green herringbone twill uniform consisting of a loose-fitting jacket cut in a similar style to the black panzer jacket, but with a large pocket on the left breast, and trousers with a large thigh pocket. The difference in shades between the two pieces is significant. He has attached his M1935 officers' collar patches on the jacket but presumably has left his shoulder boards attached to the field grey uniform underneath.

Visible in this photograph are four of the six Hummels that would typically be assigned to a battery. They have all received a solid coat of whitewash with blast residue darkening the barrel ends. Notice that the roof tarpaulin draped over the side of the nearest vehicle has a lighter colored inside compared to its exterior. Of particular interest is the unit insignia on the front superstructure, a triangle with three circles. This was the divisional emblem of 333.Infanterie-Division, and since Hummels were not assigned to infantry units and no record exists of this unit having Hummels, it is a bit of a mystery. This division was part of 1.Panzerarmee in the fall and winter of 1943, so perhaps one of the Panzer-Divisionen assigned their battery of Hummels to them for an extended period and they thus adopted their insignia, although 333.Inf.Div. was disbanded in November 1943.

This is another Hummel from the same unit as the previous photo, the triangular insignia just visible on the rear plate. It could be the vehicle in the left background based on the solid band of worn whitewash from the travel lock and the recuperator cylinder above the barrel having a more complete coating of white. The crew appear to be getting the vehicle ready to move, securing the crossbar that holds the two halves of the travel lock together. The whitewash has been very neatly applied around the white outline of the Balkenkreuz. This vehicle could be classified as "mid-production" as the end of the right-side exhaust pipe is visible above the idler, so it lacks the exhaust muffler that was discontinued in August 1943, but still has the early style of "Fahrerraum" (driver's compartment) that was replaced by a larger one in February 1944.

This Hummel is from 6.Batterie / II.Abteilung of Panzer-Artillerie-Regiment 103, part of 4.Panzer-Division, and is presumably pictured in the summer or early fall of 1943. Visible on the front superstructure is a solid white gun-in-battery letter "E", over the densely applied three-color camouflage that even extends to the travel lock. Two Bosch headlights are visible amongst the mountain of jerrycans and stowage on the glacis, some appearing to be cartridge case boxes. Given that 4.Pz-Div. received its first Hummels in May/June 1943, they would have received these early production vehicles. The barrel muzzle cap is quite distinct here with its white end and red reflector in the middle, secured to the travel lock with its leather strap. Notice both the early style S-hook and later style C-hooks hanging from the spare track. The Hummel is towing a Horch Kfz.15 Medium Uniform Personenkraftwagen (m. gl. Pkw.) while another Horch with license plate "WH-270183" passes by, flying a triangular black-white-red divisional pennant.

Seen in late 1943, these Hummels have also been associated with Panzer-Artillerie-Regiment 103, 4.Pz.Div. All the vehicles appear to be painted in solid RAL 7028 Dunkelgelb, with the furthest ones making some attempt at camouflage in the open field using wooden planks and a wicker mat. A gun-in-battery letter "E" in either black or red with a white outline can be seen on the rear door of the nearest vehicle, but this is not the same vehicle seen in the previous photo given its lack of the second headlight on the right fender, so it could be a replacement. It has the same style of muzzle cap laying on the top of the travel lock. In the foreground are two 15 cm Sprenggranate Patrone 36 high explosive shells laying on logs to keep them clean, both empty and full wicker shell containers, 15 cm cartridge casings and wooden boxes that held three cartridges each. To the right is a Tellermine laying in its own wooden shipping case.

Although little is left of this Hummel seen in Hungary in 1945, enough is still intact to determine that this was a mid-production vehicle. It still has the early driver's compartment, but no longer has the exhaust muffler, which was replaced with brackets for two spare road wheels as seen here. The solid white gun-in-battery letter "C" is on the front of the left side superstructure armor. The small box mounted on the triangular support bracket held flares for the signal pistol and the round objects on either side of the gun barrel are the tops of the equilibrators. Surprisingly, the stowage box added to the left fender seems to have survived relatively intact. The white "244" was a Russian trophy number to catalog vehicles that remained on the battlefields. This vehicle was lost in March in the vicinity of Berhida-Nádasdladány during the German withdrawal.

To provide better access to the transmission and brakes as well as giving the driver and radio operator improved vision, a new "Fahrerraum" (driver's compartment) was designed in December 1943 and introduced into production in February 1944. Both crewmen had identical vision port flaps and access hatches. In August 1944, modified "Luftansaug und Luftastritt" (cooling air intake and exhaust) openings on the superstructure sides were instituted, as the open grilles were found to allow excessive dust into the engine compartment and radiators which caused reliability issues. As such, covers were installed over the cooling air intake on the left side and the air exhaust on the right, just visible here. These Hummels could be classified as final production, with less then 20%, or about 140 vehicles, having these two features. Of interest is the hard-edged camouflage that was most likely factory applied, with all three colors quite visible on the right mudflap. A six-digit Fahrgestell Nummer is stencilled in black on the upper left corner of the lower front plate, "3207?1", which would fall within the range of the last 140 Hummels produced. The picture was taken on 11 May 1945 near Schwerin, Germany, after being captured by the US 8th Infantry Division.

This Hummel abandoned in Hungary has both of the final production features and a slightly better view is offered here of the revised air exhaust cover on the right side of the superstructure. The new driver's compartment has allowed the crew to fabricate a substantial stowage frame on the right fender. On the left side of the superstructure front is a white gun-in-battery letter "F" above another Russian trophy number "265". A faint Balkenkreuz is visible on the side and an unidentified white or yellow marking is in a black or Dunkelgrau rectangle next to the radio operator's view port, possibly a tactical symbol for a self-propelled howitzer Abteilung with a "1" next to it for 1.Batterie. Similar markings were seen on other Hummels from Panzer-Artillerie-Regiment "Feldherrnhalle"(FHH) / Pz.Div. "FHH", as were brackets on the rear superstructure side for stowing a shovel that are also visible on this vehicle. Notice the late style of drive sprocket as used on the StuG III, without a hubcap.

Number "113" in the Russian trophy list is another final production Hummel, its rear portion having been completely destroyed whereas the front is relatively intact, although the end of the barrel has taken a damaging hit. The armored cover for the brake cooling air intake is missing on the left side of the glacis and reveals the simple hole that was there. The spare tracks have been placed in the front bracket rather haphazardly, with a single link, a section of five, and then a section of eight facing the opposite direction. Once again, the late StuG III drive sprocket is used. The photo was presumably taken in the Budapest area during the siege of 1944-45, and the vehicle could belong to either Pz.Div. "FHH" or Panzer-Artillerie-Regiment 13 / 13.Pz.Div., as these were the only two units with Hummels in the vicinity.

Not much is left of this Hummel being used for a photo opportunity by an American soldier, but it does have the late production driver's compartment. Of interest here is the combination of suspension components. Four of the eight roadwheels (at stations 1, 2, 3 and 5) have the earlier cast hubcaps whereas the other four have the later pressed ones introduced into Pz.Kpfw.IV production in September 1943. The return rollers are the later steel rimmed ones that were introduced to save rubber, and the ones on either side of the G.I. have the two "spokes" whereas the first one does not. Finally, unlike many Hummels, it is equipped with tracks with a hollow guide horn. The tube sticking out of the sloped plate below the gun discharged warm air from the engine.

This Hummel, presumably belonging to Pz.Art.Reg. "FHH", was photographed on Attila Way in Budapest near the Royal Palace, with the statue of horse drawn artillery in the background in Palota Square (now Dózsa György Square). Although it has suffered catastrophic destruction, there is enough left to still identify many late production details. We know it lacked the muffler, since this change also resulted in the rear tow hooks being turned upside down (the opening facing up) as clearly seen here. The late, widened driver's compartment is just visible, as well as a steel return roller and drive sprocket without hubcap, all indicative of a vehicle produced in the fall of 1944. Furthermore, it has a feature that is seldom visible. Just below the exhaust pipe welded to the hull is the track pin return plate, meant to push loose track pins back in as they went by during travel. This was something first introduced on the Pz.Kpfw.IV Ausf.J in November 1944, so this Hummel must have built in mid-late November and sent straight to the frontline in Hungary, given that the Soviets completed their encirclement of Budapest on 26 December 1944. The vehicle would have also had the cooling air intake and exhaust modifications.

This is another Hummel lost during the siege of Budapest, in this case somewhere on the Buda side of the Danube River. It was probably knocked out by heavy artillery given the shattered armor on the left side and its position in what seems to be a shell crater. Visible on the hull rear is the upside-down tow hook so no muffler is present, and the portion of the front hatch that can be seen suggests it has the wider driver's compartment. A clearer view is provided here of the bracket and clamp for stowing a shovel on the superstructure side as seen in a previous photo, so this is probably another "Feldherrnhalle" Hummel. A Balkenkreuz in the typical FHH style and location is also faintly visible beside the torn roof tarpaulin.

Péter Kocsis

Given the Hummel's limited stowage of 18 rounds of ammunition, an ammunition resupply vehicle was essential and thus the Geschützwagen III/IV für Munition (Munitionsfahrzüge) was produced and issued on a scale of two for each battery of six Hummels. They were identical to regular Hummels, but equipped with additional ammunition racks and an armored plate covered the gun opening, allowing easy conversion to a Hummel if necessary. Thus, they exhibited similar production details such as the one seen here painted in three-color camouflage, with a single Bosch headlight, early driver's compartment, and mudflaps at the rear. It also has the earlier sprocket with its eight round holes, all features suggesting a vehicle built before June 1943. Of interest is the travel lock that was installed at the factory, as opposed to just the attachment brackets. Notice the mix of spare tracks with both solid and open guide horns.

A group of vehicles from an Artillerie-Abteilung on the move, with two Hummels in the center background, a Geschützwagen III/IV für Munition on the left and a Geschützwagen II für Munition on the right, used to resupply those batteries equipped with the 10.5cm Sd.Kfz.124 "Wespe" (Wasp), the Hummel's stablemate. All the vehicles appear to be finished in solid RAL 7028 Dunkelgelb, or perhaps whitewashed, and both Munitionsfahrzüge have a unit emblem in the shape of a shield, but it is unfortunately illegible. This Geschützwagen III/IV für Munition does not have a travel lock, but the brackets are still visible beside the armored covers over the brake cooling air intakes.

Péter Kocsis

The Somua S35 is generally considered to be the best French tank during the 1940 German invasion, having a good combination of firepower (47mm SA35 gun), armor (40mm at the front capable of withstanding hits from the Pak 36 3.7 cm anti-tank gun) and speed (average of 35kph). However, it still suffered from a small turret and overworked commander, along with antiquated French tactics. This vehicle with "matricule" (registration number) "M848" is from 4ème Régiment de Cuirassiers, 1ère Division Légère Mécanique (4th Regiment, 1st Light Mechanized Division) and belonged to the commander of 1er Escadron (1st Squadron), Captain de Segonzac, so lacks a turret number. Due to being a command vehicle it was one of the few that had radio equipment, hence the antenna on the front right corner with the unique style of French "concertina" insulator. The symbol for the 4th Regiment is behind it, a white Joan of Arc on horseback overtop a red shield with white outline. It was lost on Rue Coulon in Jolimetz, France on 18 May 1940 with the Église Saint-Pierre de Jolimetz cathedral in the background. The camouflage is quite distinct consisting of horizontal stripes outlined in black, the three colors most likely being Terre D'ombre (red brown), Vert Foncé (dark green) and Vert Olive Clair (light olive green).

Péter Kocsis

This S35 with solid white turret number "32" and matricule "M10741" got stuck in a ditch on the road between Jauche and Émines (part of Namur), Belgium on 13 May 1940 while conducting a fighting retreat and taking a number of hits. It is from 1ère Régiment de Cuirassiers, 3ère Division Légère Mécanique (DLM) and was commanded by Second Lieutenant Issaverdens, commander of 2e Peloton (2nd Platoon) of the 2e Escadron. The pillaging has already started, with all the straps on the side bins undone to gain access and one already on the ground, and a rear engine access door open with two engine starter handles laying on it. This vehicle carries one of the more distinctive camouflage patterns of very wavy, twisty shapes outlined with very thin black lines. A minimum of four colors were used although five was common – one "shading" tone Terre D'ombre, two "ground" tones Vert Foncé and Vert Olive Clair, and two "sky" tones Gris Bleu Clair (light grey blue) and Gris Clair Neutre (Neutral Light Grey). Notice the very pronounced casting numbers on the hull side and doors, and the prominent cast "SOMUA" plate below the fishtails of the exhaust.

Recognizing that the S35 could be a useful addition to the Wehrmacht, collection of useable vehicles began, including this Somua already marked with white outline Balkenkreuz being used to tow another. The new owners have also painted out the French license plate below the cast "SOMUA" plate, but both vehicles retain their French camouflage. Although the second is somewhat indistinct, both appear to have yet another different style, with the hull painted with three colors of horizontal stripes edged in black, while the turret has wavy blotches in the same three colors and also outlined in black. The Somua it is towing with matricule "M10716" is the platoon commander's tank from 3e Peloton, 2e Escadron of the 2ème Régiment de Cuirassiers, 3ère DLM. While the solid white turret numbers "86" appear to have black outlines, they do not. Once again, casting numbers are quite prominent on the hull sides and access doors of both vehicles. The towing operation appears to have caused mechanical problems given the open engine door.

Salvaging efforts also including using German equipment such as this 12-ton Sd.Kfz.8 DB9 halftrack with the familiar Daimler-Benz 3-pointed star emblem on its sprocket hub, stowed with a number of tow cables and spare road wheel. It is towing a 20-ton French tank transport trailer, built by either Titan or Coder, with each DLM typically having a repair squadron equipped with twelve to move its S35s. This Somua, matricule "M838", is from the 13ème Régiment de Dragons (RD), 2ème DLM. Identification of platoons and squadrons was done via "les as" (the aces), as the playing card symbols were referred to. In this case it is a blue heart with white outline on the forward turret side, signifying the 2e Peloton of 1e Escadron and although not seen, this S35 carried white turret number "10". Somuas were not known for carrying names in any unit, but the platoons of 1st squadron did exactly that, and barely visible above the "SOMUA" nameplate on the glacis is "Le Léopard" (The Leopard) in white. All four side bins have already been removed.

Péter Kocsis

Two Somuas are examined by German soldiers that were abandoned by their crews in the Dunkirk sector of France. Both are from the 18ème Régiment de Dragons, the other unit within 1ème DLM equipped with S35s. This unit used a more unique marking system as seen on white "81" with matricule " 67240", the M being excluded in this case. The white heart still identified the 2e Peloton, while the solid blue circle with the white hippogriffe regimental insignia identified the 4e Escadron. "64" is from the 3e Peloton of 1e Escadron, this squadron using a similar marking system but having their aces in solid blue with a white outline. 64 carried a diamond. Its matricule was "M886" and it carries an unusual dark-colored upside-down heart on its cupola, no doubt a personal insignia; another 18ème RD Somua had a small duck on its hull. The three-color horizontal striped camouflage is quite distinct here on the turret of 64.

Péter Kocsis

The abundance of captured French tanks along with the ability to repair them at the French depots and factories that built them meant that the Wehrmacht was quick to take them into use. Approximately 300 Somua S35s saw service on virtually ever front and locale that the Wehrmacht fought in. Units composed entirely of "beutepanzers" (booty tanks) were already established by the end of 1940. This Somua in the process of being loaded onto a rail car belonged to Panzer-Kompanie 223 which was established in France in February 1942 with five S35s and twenty-two Hotchkiss H39. It was eventually sent to Heeresgruppe Süd (Army Group South) later in the year and attached to 22.Pz.Div, fighting with its beutepanzers in the Crimea for the rest of 1942 and into 1943. The Somua has been re-painted in RAL 7021 Dunkelgrau and the letters "CO" or "GO" are on the turret, of unknown meaning but perhaps referring to the unit commander.

Péter Kocsis

Panzer-Regiment 201 was one of the first beutepanzer units created, in mid-December 1940, consisting of two Abteilungs with three companies each. Each company had five Somua S35 and twelve Hotchkiss H39, designated Pz.Kpfw.35S and Pz.Kpfw.38H in German service. Seen in this photo are three Somua and two Hotchkiss, still with the original French cupolas, the only exterior changes being a coat of RAL 7021 Dunkelgrau and new markings. The turret numbers are in white outline and "101" would be the first of two Somuas in the Kompanie-Trupp (HQ) of 1.Kompanie. The next Somua is "121" and the Hotchkiss between them "122", so the first and second vehicles in the 2.Zug (2nd Platoon) of 1.Kompanie. The farthest Somua appears to have "111" so it is from 1.Zug. The variation in Balkenkreuz is interesting, with the nearest vehicle having a thicker black cross as well as a black outline around the white portions. Notice the prominent "HOTCHKISS" plate on the nearest vehicle. A year later, Pz.Rgt.201 would be assigned to 23.Pz.Div.

After the fall of France and the establishment of the Vichy government, the only tank units left under French control were those located in the overseas colonies, particularly in Africa and the Middle East. The Germans allowed them to keep these forces in place to help control Free French and British intentions and were even convinced to allow them to create a new tank unit using 23 Somua S35s and support vehicles sent from France. Receiving their equipment in Senegal in July 1941, they became the 2e Escadron of the 12ème Groupement Autonome des Chasseurs d'Afrique (GACA). The Somuas were numbered consecutively using large white turret numbers with black outlines, so "2" was the second tank in the 1e Peloton, hence the ace of spades marking. It is not clear what color the aces were, since the 2nd squadron should have used white, although this very dusty vehicle appears to only have the "spade" in black outline. Although not visible here, the matricule for this S35 was "M50318".

Images Défense

The Somuas first arrived in Morocco in December 1940 where they were refurbished despite the best efforts of the German control commission to render them barely serviceable prior to shipping. It was presumably at this time that they were repainted in more appropriate camouflage, but it is difficult to discern if this was two or three colors and which tones were actually used, but possibly Ocre Jaune (Yellow Ochre), Vert Olive (Olive Green) and Ocre Rouge (Red Ochre), or perhaps locally sourced paints. After joining the Allied side and being reorganized, the 12ème GACA became the 12ème Régiment de Chasseurs d'Afrique (RCA) and the S35s became the 7e Escadron, fighting in Tunisia between March and May 1943, losing four Somuas to combat action. Tank "8" was in the 2e Peloton and thus used the ace of hearts. The aces symbols were probably red (with a white outline) given that it was the 7th squadron. On the first two side stowage bins a large blue/white/red French tricolor was painted, which was repeated on the opposite side crew door.

This is another picture of Somua "8" as the crew undertakes track and suspension maintenance. The matricule "M50324" can be seen and to the left of the radio operator/loader's vision port the 12ème RCA insignia is barely visible, consisting of a white stylized horse standing on its hind legs superimposed over the African continent in red, surrounded by a notched white ring. Carrying a length of spare track on the glacis was also a common fixture on many of the Somuas in Tunisia. In the background is tank "9"; turret numbers were carried on both turret sides as well as on the commander's rear turret hatch, with the aces on both sides in front of the vehicle number. The other rear turret side beside the hatch had the French red/white/blue roundel painted on it, which was also repeated on top of the cupola, although this was changed to a white Allied star on some of the S35s.

Since there were five tanks in each platoon, Somua "10" was the last tank in the 2e Peloton, hence it still has the red ace of hearts symbol. A better view is provided here of the French tricolor on the stowage bins, the crew using the spot for the missing fourth bin to stow some personal gear. A length of spare track is also carried on the glacis. Although dusty, much of the camouflage pattern can be discerned, consisting of random splotches and squiggles, similar to what might be seen on post-1942 German armored vehicles.

A look at Somua "10" from the rear, with its tactical number on the commander's turret hatch visible along with the matricule "M50289". A French roundel was also carried on the rear plate below the exhaust, but it is covered here by the crew stowage. The towing chains were a common fixture on most French tanks as these were usually factory supplied with each vehicle. Many of the Somuas in the 12ème RCA seemed to be equipped with radios as evidenced by the antenna mounted here with the concertina insulator covered, perhaps to help keep dust away from the electrical connection. The tank commander still wears the original Model 1935 motorised troops' helmet.

ADOC-photos

During the Paris uprising in August 1944, members of the Forces Francaises de l'intérieur (FFI / French Forces of the Interior) resistance found an abandoned S35 at the SOMUA works, finished in German three color camouflage and equipped with the modified cut down cupola and split hatch, along with a German style antenna mount as seen here. Although it lacked ammunition, it was used throughout the liberation as a status symbol, adorned with white crosses of Lorraine and French tricolors on all four sides of the vehicle and the turret. The markings partially overpainted the German tactical number "734" in yellow on the turret, whereas the white "G29" on the glacis is of unknown origin and could have been applied by the FFI.

ADOC-photos

The Somua was originally named "Mounette" but at some point, presumably at the end of the uprising on August 23, it was parked in front of the Batignolles town hall in the 17th Arrondissement (borough) of Paris and the name was overpainted with "Batignolles" seen here. The small French tricolor on the front below the name was replaced with a much larger version and "FFI" was added to both hull sides. Furthermore, white graffiti was applied, reading "L'ALLEMAGNE comme CARTHAGE sera DETRUITE" (Germany like Carthage will be Destroyed) on the turret and "L'ALLEMAGNE comme CARTHAGE sera, Tout de même, DETRUITE signé H.Dupius" (Germany, like Carthage, will be destroyed all the same signed H.Paquis) on the front plate. "EPINETTES" (Spruce) also appears but its meaning is unclear. Notice the French flag flying from the cupola with the 17th Arrondissement text and the sandbagged position on the roof in the background.

These two Somua S35s knocked out on a road in Finland between Kemi and Tornio appear to have been damaged by mines. They belong to Panzer-Abteilung 211, which was part of Kampfgruppe Tornio that was fighting to recapture the bridges at Tornio between 2 – 6 October 1944, after these were taken by the Finnish following their armistice with the Soviets in September and pressure from their new allies to start serious hostilities with the Germans. The Somuas were probably lost in the initial attack on October 3. The sign reads "Jätteille" which in Finnish means a place for garbage or waste, so it is definitely a bit appropriate!

This picture taken from the other side shows to better effect the damaged track on the left side. The Somua may have suffered an internal explosion give the lack of turret cupola, the side door barely hanging on to its hinge and an engine grille lying next to the right side seen in the previous photo. Pz.Abt.211 was formed in Finland in March 1941 and entered combat in July, seeing continual action for a couple of months and then spending 1942 to September 1944 quietly in a defensive role in Karelia. It consisted of 2 companies and a staff company, equipped with 16 Pz.Kpfw.35S and 26 Pz.Kpfw.38H.

During the fighting around Tornio, most of Pz.Abt.211's tanks appear to have been covered with a coating of mud that is clearly seen here. There is some suggestion that this may have been an attempt at Zimmerit, and there is a pattern seen on the right side of the lower front plate. Many of the Pz.Kpfw.35S and Pz.Kpfw.38H seem to have been painted in RAL 7028 Dunkelgelb with traces of a camouflage pattern in RAL 6003 Olivgrün and/or RAL 8017 Rotbraun so if this was a coating of mud it may have been a way to better blend in with the darker terrain of Finland in autumn. This picture was taken at a later date then the previous two, as the spare track is no longer on the glacis which provides a good look at the simple hooks that were used. The driver's vision port cover plate has also been opened.

This is a rear view of the same Somua with the open side door seeming to show the camouflage to good effect. The mud covering extends down the hull and turret sides, but the rear of the hull and turret have been left uncoated. Most of the tanks in Pz.Abt.211 carried additional stowage boxes and bins on the rear hull such as seen here, with a unit fabricated metal box to the right and what appears to be a wooden ammunition crate on the left. The opening for the rear right engine grate, seen lying next to the tank in one of the previous photos, is visible here and one of the engine access hatches is open, causing the tank commander's turret hatch to swivel backwards into the turret. Even after four years a section of the tow chain is still in place!

The rear Somua appears to be in a bit better condition then the front one, only having lost one track and appearing to be relatively intact. It also has rear mounted stowage bins, a metal one mounted on the rear plate with a wooden crate attached, as well as another wooden bin to the right. An attempt has been made to use pine boughs as foliage camouflage and it to seems to have a coating of mud, although not as dense as the other Somua.

This photo was again taken at a later date, and it appears that much of the mud has been washed off by rain and the foliage has disappeared. This suggests that it was in fact mud or some other type of removable coating. Both the wooden bin and crate have been taken, revealing the metal bin that was a standardised design in this unit. Remnants of a camouflage pattern can be seen. The split hatches of the German modified cupola have also been opened up along with the side door and some of the unique Somua square handles attached to the side access doors have been taken. By November, Pz.Abt.211 had retreated to Norway and been brought back up to strength with 15 Somuas by combining it with other beutepanzer units defending Norway.